FOREVER FLOWERS

£2.50

FOREVER FLOWERS

JOANNA SHEEN

CLB

Colour Library Books

CLB 4563
This edition published 1996
by Colour Library Books

Set in Life by SX Composing Ltd,
Rayleigh, Essex
Printed and bound in Singapore
by Tien Wah Press
ISBN 1-85833-524-8

Contents

Introduction

Flowers are amongst the most beautiful of mother nature's creations and the pleasure that they are able to give, whether in a garden or in displays around the house, is immense.

Although fresh flowers and plants have an intrinsic beauty that nothing can ever surpass, there are times and places when man-made imitations can also give a huge amount of satisfaction. There are so many instances when fresh flowers would either be impractical or too expensive, and this is where artificial flowers and foliage can star in their own right.

In years gone by, the image of silk or fabric flowers was very poor, and conjured up images of a couple of overly bright yellow daffodils gracing the table of a dull restaurant in the middle of summer! Cheap plastic roses and unrecognizable fantasy flowers are a world away from the wonderful and very lifelike creations that are available today. Given plenty of inspiration and a reasonable budget you can create some fantastic displays and arrangements that will grace your home for ever – or at least until you are fed up with them and want to turn them into a totally new decoration. Silk flowers can be used and re-used dozens of times in different arrangements.

It is probably best to start with one of the less ambitious projects in the book, experimenting with a small selection of artificial flowers and foliage in order to get a feel for working with them. There are many advantages to working with artificial flowers when compared to arranging fresh flowers – there is no water for instance, so no drips. There are no stems or leaves to be trodden underfoot and stain the flooring. Artificial flowers are also far cleaner than dried flowers, which although glorious in their own right, do make the most horrendous mess on the way between bunch and basket! I would suggest using a little artifice, in that it may not be advisable to display flowers that are out of season – we're back to the two sad daffodils in the middle of summer! Try to make sure that your

RIGHT: This beautiful selection of traditional cottage garden flowers includes some foxgloves, scabious and cosmos, small lilies, bells of Ireland and clematis. They are simply tied with a beautiful ribbon.

LEFT: The dramatic beauty of the clematis flower is brought indoors to create an unusual set of bookends.

display is either multi-seasonal or appropriate for the current season. Also, replace your displays occasionally to ring the changes.

BELOW: This charming photograph frame shows how just a few flowers can transform an ordinary object into a delightful home accessory.

Silk flowers need a minimal amount of looking after. They will give you many years of pleasure and decoration and in return only need a little careful dusting, and when they seem to be getting really grubby, a wash or wipe. If your arrangement is made up with a glue gun and uses flower heads only, a careful wipe with a damp cloth and, if necessary, a little washing up liquid will suffice. If, however, you have a larger arrangement that is based in florist's foam, then once a year or so it is worth dismantling it and individually washing the flowers and leaves in a little warm, soapy water and then drying them with a soft cloth. This restores the flowers to their pristine beauty and will make them look as good as new again, giving you years more to admire them.

TECHNIQUES

EQUIPMENT

You only need a minimum amount of equipment when working with artificial flowers. A really tough pair of florist's scissors is a must, with a section designed for cutting wires. You also need an extremely efficient pair of pliers or wire cutters. Wires and tape are sometimes necessary, depending on the project. Also required is florist's foam suitable for dried flowers as well as silk flowers. In an emergency you can use the variety that is intended for fresh flower arrangements, but do not add water. One of the most essential pieces of equipment for many of the projects is the hot glue gun. These can be bought from craft and hardware stores and are used in almost every case to attach the fruit and flowers as the adhesive dries rather quickly. However, remember that you have only 15 seconds to position the pieces before the bond is made.

PREPARING THE FLOWERS

1 When you purchase artificial flowers, you might find that they are squashed and flattened, and sometimes almost unrecognizable as the flowers they are meant to be. This is easily remedied, and with a little art and ingenuity they will soon look amazingly lifelike. The petals are usually wired and can therefore be bent and twisted in all directions. Unfurl the petals to give the flower a more realistic look. Smooth out some petals and perhaps add a slight twist to others, so that they are not over-perfect, which can also detract from the realistic look.

2 Use pliers or wirecutters to cut the stems of flowers down to size. Some of the larger stems are unbelievably tough, and trying to wrench a piece off the bottom of a thick wire stem is very frustrating indeed.

3 The stems are usually completely straight, and as this almost never happens in nature, it improves the look of the flower or piece of foliage if you gently bend and twist the stem to add a little extra realism. It can take some time to turn each carefully packaged piece into a perfect shape. Allow a reasonable amount of time, especially if you are working on a large project. It is, however, time extremely well spent as the difference between a package of rigid and flattened "soldiers" and some natural, twisty flowers and stems is amazing.

TYING A BOW

1 One of the most invaluable additions to artificial flowers is a ribbon trim. You can tie traditional bows, as you would tie your shoelaces, or you can achieve a far quicker, much more professional finish by using the method demonstrated in these steps. The length of ribbon you will require is dependent upon the size of the finished bow that you need, so some practice in gauging the length of ribbon may be necessary. For an average size bow, take about a 45 cm (18 in) length of ribbon. Holding on to one end of the ribbon, wrap the other end around as though you were wrapping a shawl around someone's shoulders and hold in the middle as shown in the photograph.

2 Once you are happy that the ends are equal and that the loops are the right length, take a piece of medium-gauge florist's wire and wrap it tightly around the middle of the loops, scrunching up the ribbon as you wrap the wire around. This creates a perfect bow, and once you have mastered the technique, it takes far less time than a traditional bow and gives a flatter, better result.

DECORATIVE DISPLAYS

All the projects in this section are designed to give you new or unusual ideas for arrangements and displays around your home. Often a very large fresh flower arrangement might only last a week or so despite the enormous cost involved, whereas these silk flower ideas will last as long as you need them. Once you want to change things around, then they can easily be converted into a completely new arrangement – flowers forever!

PAINTED FLOWERS

The wonderful displays and selections of flowers chosen by the Old Masters as subjects for their paintings were the inspiration for this project. There are various star ingredients such as lilies or tulips that appeared in the old paintings time and time again, and once you have worked with them in arrangements you will appreciate why the artists loved their shape and colour so much.

Equipment: *large container – at least 40 cm (15 in) high; 2 blocks florist's foam.*
Flowers and fruit: *5 stems ivy; 5 stems pink lilac; 5 stems rubrum lily; 5 stems white wild roses; 5 stems black grapes; 3 stems each pears, lemons and apples.*

1 Choose a container that has plenty of width at the neck. A deep bowl could work well or a large ceramic pot. Metals are also suitable for this type of display, so copper, pewter or brass would all be possible candidates. Once you have chosen your container, fill it with foam. If it is an open bowl then tape the foam in position. If it is a ceramic container, as in this example, make sure the foam comes well up to the top or you will waste height filling the vase with stems. Place some trails of ivy leaves to come over the edge of the container and put some sprays of lilac in position.

2 Add in all the remaining sprays of lilac, making sure that they are well spaced over the arrangement. Carefully open and unfurl some of the lilies and place them in the centre of the arrangement. Many varieties of lily are available in silk, and those shown here are just one example of a range of colours and effects. You could choose a plainer cream, pink or red lily.

3 Once all the lilies are in position, place some of the sprays of cream wild roses into the foam. These should be left as clusters rather than cut down and used individually as they make a far greater impact when put into the arrangement *en masse*. Again, many other colours are available and you might like to add a much stronger colour to your design.

4 The final touch is the fruit. This comes conveniently wired on to stems, so can be pushed straight into the arrangement, unlike the real thing that takes quite a bit of preparation! Trim the stems if necessary as the fruit needs to sit well within the flowers rather than standing out too far. The fruit used here all have a crackle finish, which was how they were supplied. You could easily add a crackle glaze to standard fruit to give a little more of the 'Old Master' feel to the arrangement!

1

3

2

4

Left: Sometimes flowers are not needed for a display. This bowl of crackle-finish fruit echoes the fresh fruit in the oil painting behind.

Right: This magnificent display would last such a short time if you used real fruits and flowers – perhaps only long enough to paint it and create a permanent record in that way! This artificial version looks quite beautiful, and after the initial expenditure on the ingredients can be admired as long as an Old Master painting!

Terrific Topiary

Fairy-tale topiary trees made with pansies are only possible using silk flowers – the fresh variety would quickly wilt. Artificial twigs give a wonderful wild feel to the trees. Unfurl them carefully and bend and twist them into position.

Flowers and stems: *artificial twigs; pansies in your choice of colours; a few stems of ivy.*
Equipment: *terracotta base, cement or plaster, and a stick for each tree; 1 ball florist's foam for each tree (here we used a 7 cm (2¾ in), a 9 cm (3½ in) and a 12 cm (4¾ in) ball); some extra florist's foam.*

1 The first step is to organize some containers. These are terracotta pots that have been painted with a granite finish. The stick is then placed in the centre of the pot and held in position while cement or plaster is poured around it. Do not fill the pot right to the top as it needs to have a little dry foam covering the cement in which to arrange the flowers. Once the cement is dry, cover the base cement with a little foam and press a suitably sized ball on to the stick. The artificial twigs are added next. Carefully twist and unfurl them and place the central stem down into the base foam. Then squash and twist them into a wonderfully wild design as pictured in the photograph.

2 It is simplest to decorate the base first while there are no flowers in the top ball to get in the way. Place some ivy leaves, pansy foliage and pansy flowers throughout the base to cover it well. Some of the ivy could climb up the twisted stems to meet some ivy trailing down from the top ball. Make sure that none of the foam is visible when the base is finished and that there is a good coverage of greenery and colour.

3 Then begin the top. Place several ivy leaves and sprays of ivy in position first; the ivy can stick out beyond the flowers. The overall effect intended for these topiary trees is a fairy-tale colour scheme but with wild wood undertones! Add in plenty of pansy leaves of various sizes. Pansies are available in small, medium and large sizes and a mixture of these is excellent. Whether you choose to mix colours is completely up to you.

4 Finally finish decorating the ball with any left-over pansy flowers, making sure again that no grey foam is visible as this spoils the whole tree. Obviously on a larger tree, the larger size of pansy will look more suitable, and similarly on the smaller tree the tinier viola and other pansy varieties can be more successful.

LEFT: These topiary trees in fairy-tale colours would look charming in any room setting. The artificial twigs are very unusual and exciting ingredients to use and the pansies really do look extremely lifelike.

DELPHINIUMS AND CLEMATIS

This collection of flowers usually seen only in a summer garden can grace your fireplace all year round. Fresh clematis would not be happy or last long in an arrangement of this kind. Durability is one of the most important bonuses of using silk flowers.

Flowers, vegetables and fruit: *3 stems white/cream delphiniums; 3–5 stems grey or green foliage; 5 stems blue/purple clematis; 5 stems wild artichokes; 5 stems sloe berries and foliage.*
Equipment: *tall container; 1 block florist's foam.*

1 If the container has a fairly narrow neck, then place a suitably sized piece of foam into the neck and wedge it tightly into position. If necessary you could also tape this in place to be doubly sure that it will not move. Then begin to cover the foam with some sprays of summer foliage in shades of grey as used here or some green. The foliage should fall down over the sides of the vase, as well as standing up from the arrangement, to add softness and form.

2 Place the delphiniums in next, as they have fairly thick stems and you need plenty of room in the foam to accommodate them. Make sure that you have played with the wired stems a little before using them and tease them into a

LEFT: The real version of this arrangement would simply not be possible as most of us would be unwilling to denude our clematis plants, and the chances of this many perfect flowers would probably be minimal!

few bends and curves as very few delphiniums are ramrod straight – apart from those raised by the really expert grower no doubt! Give the stems a little movement and place them towards the back of the arrangement.

3 The clematis need quite a bit of work before they are placed into a display. Unfurl all the petals and bend the leaves, stems and buds in varying directions to give a lifelike feel to the flower. Place sprays of clematis to the right of the arrangement and to the bottom left, and have one small spray trailing over the edge of the vase at the bottom right-hand side of the group.

4 Trim and add the pieces of wild artichoke. These are very attractive and fairly easy to include in arrangements as they are somewhat smaller than the standard edible artichoke, which can only take centre stage in a display. Use some of the artichokes individually, and leave some in their sprays of two or three. Fill the gaps to the right of the group with artichokes and have them coming through the centre of the flowers to the bottom left-hand side. Finally, add the sprigs of blue sloe berries. These are a perfect colour to complement the clematis, and add a little detail and interest to the display.

A Basket of Trailing Hops and Roses

Hanging baskets are a welcome sight in the summer, gracing many doorways and gates, patios and barbecue areas. This hanging basket is designed for use inside and adds a splash of colour in a position that might not be possible with fresh flowers.

Flowers: *5 lengths hop vine with flowers; 5 stems pink blossom; 7 stems pink wild roses with foliage.*

Equipment: *metal hanging basket; 2 blocks florist's foam; fabric to drape around basket; cord to hang basket, if required.*

It is essential to decide on the exact position in which you want to hang the basket, as it is much easier to adjust the length of the cords or chains at this point than to fiddle with them later. Once you have organized the correct length for the chains, then you can cover the basket.

1 A square piece of fabric quite a bit larger than the basket is ideal. Stand the basket in the middle of the square of

1

LEFT: This lovely hanging basket is probably quicker to construct than the usual garden variety, and does not cry out nightly to be watered. This display will give you pleasure for many more months than the outdoor flower basket, so why not try making one? An old hanging basket frame could be used and some spare material or a remnant would be sufficient to cover the base.

fabric and bring the corners over to the inside. These can be fixed with pins, glue or tape, but safety pins are probably the easiest way to secure the material. Once the fabric is fairly taut and the outside of the basket completely hidden, you can fill the basket with florist's foam. This should be taped into position using florist's tape, if you have it, or masking tape. Make sure the tape will be well hidden once the arrangement is complete.

2 Separate some of the foliage from the hops and place the leaves fairly low in the basket. These will need to mask the grey foam to ensure none is visible in the finished display. You can then add some longer trails of hops and allow them to cascade over the edge of the basket. The hop flowers are so attractive that it is worth placing them on the overhanging trails rather than in the mass of the basket, so that they can be appreciated rather than lost in with the other flowers.

3 Once the overall shape of the basket has been formed and the trailing hops are in position, you must add the wild roses. These will probably need to be cut down as they are usually on a fairly long stem. Use some of them individually and others in sprays of two or three, and include all their foliage. Do make sure that there is a good spread of roses throughout the arrangement, unless it is hanging in a tight corner and you wish to leave the back a little emptier.

4 Finally, add the blossom sprays. These are usually far larger than you would need for a project of this size and will have to be cut into smaller sprays. This is not difficult and just means wielding the pliers and wire-cutting scissors. Tuck in small but bold bunches of the berries between all the flowers to give a frothy and delicate look to the finished basket arrangement.

TROPICAL SPLENDOUR

These wonderful arum lilies could add a warm, exotic and tropical feel to a corner of any suitable room. The composition of the arrangement is simplicity itself and, as with all silk flowers, barring a little dusting now and again, will give you pleasure for many years.

Flowers: *3 green/yellow arum lilies; 4 orange/flame red arum lilies; 1 stem orange/brown trailing vine.*
Equipment: *bamboo containers or similar; 1 block florist's foam.*

1 The bamboo containers here were actually bought in Japan last time I was there, which I realize is of little help to readers without access to such sources. However, the basic shape is very simple and the entire concept easy to copy with materials available in many countries. If you cannot get hold of some bamboo to cut, then any hollow dried flower stems could be used, together with two plain wooden containers. One container is filled with florist's foam and the other holds the bundle of bamboo stems cut at an angle.

2 Trim the end of the vine and stick it into the foam so that the leaves trail up and over the edge of the container. Position the second bundle of bamboo over a little of the vine to help keep it in position. Place the three green lilies into the foam, having trimmed them to different lengths for a triangular shape.

RIGHT: The interesting contrasts of shape and colour make this arrangement really intriguing. As it is such a strong arrangement, a hallway or reception area might be a perfect position for it.

3 The other lilies are then trimmed and added into the foam at varying heights. The particular placing of the flowers is not really crucial. Do not overlap one on top of another; make sure every bloom is clearly visible. If necessary, adjust the vine leaves to make sure that the florist's foam is hidden from sight.

An alternative way of using these flowers is to hang them on a wall in a spray. The stems can be wired together with the lilies cut to varying lengths. The vine is then wound around the spray, with occasional leaves helping to disguise the wires. The trailing nature of the vine makes it simple to attach to the flowers.

Flowers and the Seashore

Some plants and flowers flourish in the heavy, steamy atmosphere of the shower room or bathroom. But all artificial flowers and plants are happy to be in any room of the house – another point scored for silk flowers!

Equipment: *wire basket; selection of 7–10 medium and large shells.*
Flowers: *12 stems wood anemones; 7 allium heads; 7 stems pale blue scillas.*

1 The wood anemones will have to be cut down a little as you need short stubby flowers or sprays for this basket. Using an all-purpose glue and a hot glue gun, attach the flowers to the mesh of the basket. It is easier to start at one point on the basket and fill the space with various flowers, rather than sticking all the

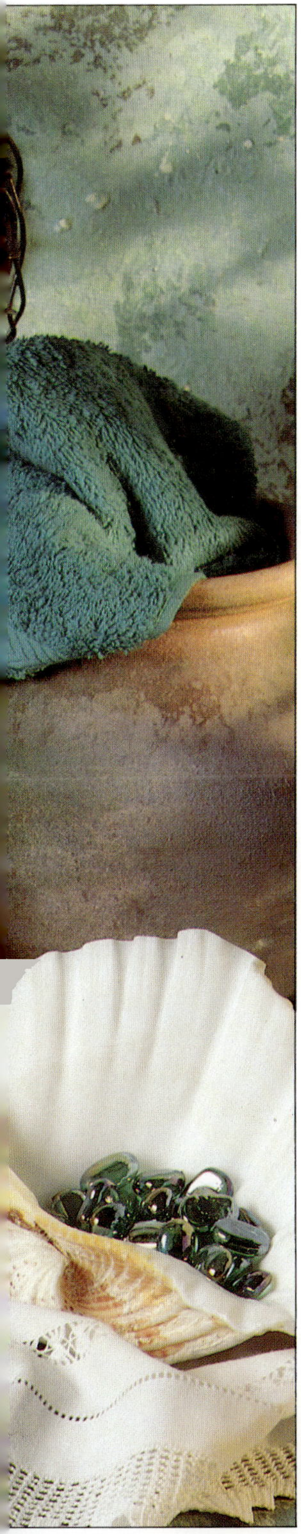

ABOVE: To complement the wire basket in the bathroom, a shell that is too large to use as part of that project is filled with a little piece of foam and a few wild flowers.

LEFT: This pretty marine-inspired basket contains a collection of sponges and shells. The wild flowers on the rim of the wire basket are all glued on with a hot glue gun that makes very light work of the project.

flowers of one variety on at once. So attach some wood anemones and some of their foliage, some scillas and an allium head on to the basket.

2 The shells should be attached to the basket at random intervals around the circumference, so once you have attached several pieces of foliage and some flowers, add a shell or two. Larger shells look wonderfully dramatic and are less likely to get lost amongst the flowers than very small shells, and although they are harder to come by, you will need fewer of them. Then add more of the foliage and flowers, travelling on around the basket.

3 Make sure that the wire base is well covered, with an even amount of flowers of all the varieties all the way round. Obviously if you know where you are going to display this basket and wish to cut back a little on the number of flowers, you could just decorate the back of the basket with foliage and place flowers at the front where they will show.

4 Continue all around the basket, adding shells of different varieties into the gaps as they appear.

A PROVENÇAL KITCHEN

These wonderfully cheerful sunflowers add a bright, sunny touch to your kitchen whether you are in Provence or Peking, Perth or Paris.

Flowers and twigs: *9 medium size sunflowers; 1 stem artificial twigs.*
Equipment: *1 wicker drinks coaster; 1 hank of raffia; yellow paper ribbon.*

1 Place all the flowers together in a bunch as shown in the photograph and wind the wired stem from one of the flowers around all the others to hold them firmly in position.

2 Use an all-purpose glue and a hot glue gun to attach the base of the stems to a wicker mat. As an alternative you could use a piece of cork or card. Take a stem of artificial twigs and bend them around the central stem of sunflowers so that they wind around the base and up the stem towards the leaves. Glue the bottom of the spiral of twigs firmly on to the wicker or cork base. Take care not to use too much glue, or it may leak out and spoil the finished effect.

3 Take the hank of green or natural coloured raffia and wind that, like a thick cord, around the central stems as a continuation of the twigs. This gives the effect of the sunflowers being contained in a cylindrical vase made from attractive natural materials.

4 As a final touch, tie a bow using yellow paper ribbon and either tie it around the stems or attach it with a hot glue gun. This finishes the container and adds a decorative touch to the arrangement. Alternatively, you could make the bow from matching raffia.

RIGHT: Often flower arrangements need quite a few ingredients to get a really special result. Here a bright, cheerful sunflower display can be created with only nine flowers and a little ingenuity.

3

1

2

4

Spring Flowers

Spring flowers are amongst the most delicate and most beautiful, but sadly not the longest lasting, of plants. Using very realistic artificial flowers you can have spring flowers in pots around the house, in perfect bloom for many weeks, or months if you want, instead of their usual short time.

Flowers and plants: *moss to cover the foam; few sprays of ivy; 12 stems of narcissi; gardener's string and narrow pieces of dowel (alternatively, use spare stalks from other silk flowers)*
Equipment: *rectangular basket approximately 30 cm (12 in) x 10 cm (4 in); 2 blocks florist's foam.*

1 The long rectangular basket is vaguely reminiscent of a window box, which adds to the atmosphere created by this display. The basket should be filled with foam, which can be wedged into position and therefore needs no extra fixings. Cover the foam roughly with moss, then fix the moss in position with pieces of stub wire bent over like hairpins. The moss should not cover the foam too heavily or it will be impossible to push any stalks into the foam. Next, scatter a few short stems of ivy through the moss, and have a few pieces trailing down over the edge of the basket.

2 The narcissi should then be placed into the arrangement in groups, as though they had been planted in that manner. Here I have used three groups each containing four stems.

3 Finish placing all the flowers into position, then push some lengths of green or brown dowelling around the clumps, as though you were intending to stake the plants to stop them breaking. Finally, wind string loosely between the stakes until you achieve the effect shown in the photograph. This display will now last all through the spring and until you wish to dismantle it.

The other spring displays are even simpler to achieve; you just need a selection of terracotta or wicker containers. Fill them with foam and cover this with moss in the same way as in the main project. These can then be filled with the spring bulbs of your choice.

Left: There are many varieties of spring flower that could look wonderful given similar treatment: tulips, daffodils, bluebells, crocuses and forget-me-nots to name but a few.

Far right: Bring a touch of spring indoors for a few weeks or months with this bright display of narcissi. The moss stakes and string makes for surprising realism.

ORNAMENTAL FLOWERS

Now you can add to the excitement of floral decoration by using artificial flowers to embellish items in your home. Transform plain bookends, lamps, candlesticks and bowls into unusual and attractive home accessories and let silk and parchment flowers of the highest quality take centre stage on stunning firescreens, candelabras and even chandeliers.

WHITEWASHED FRUITBOWL

This unusual pastel effect is created from a plain ceramic bowl, a selection of artificial fruit, a little white emulsion paint and some creamy yellow emulsion paint. It takes a little time and is rather fiddly but is great fun to create.

Fruit: *selection of grapes, peaches, apples, pears and cherries.*
Equipment: *large ceramic bowl; white emulsion paint; yellow/cream emulsion; natural sponges.*

1 First tackle the bowl and paint it with two coats of white emulsion. If it is a darker colour to start with it may take three coats. While the bowl is drying start painting the fruit. Use the same white emulsion but instead of applying it with a brush, dab some onto a natural sponge and press the sponge all over the fruit. The intention is to cover the fruit with a coating of white emulsion but to allow some of the natural colour to peep through. It sometimes helps to put a fair amount of paint onto the fruit and then use a piece of kitchen paper to wipe some away again. Some of the smaller pieces of fruit – the cherries perhaps, should be left their natural colour to add a flash of colour to the display. When the bowl is completely dry use a clean sponge dabbed in the yellow/cream paint and dot that over the bowl to tone down the brilliant white effect.

2 Once all the fruit has been painted and both the bowl and fruit are dry you can start on your creation! Begin with a spray of grapes and a couple of large fruit to make a good base for the smaller pieces. Attach them securely with your hot glue gun.

3 Build on this base by adding more grapes and another couple of the plainer large fruit like the apples or pears. It is much easier to add the small pieces at the end than the larger ones. The spray of fruit should be beginning to take shape now. The grapes used here came complete with a couple of leaves and these are very useful for hiding unsightly joins. So if the fruit you are using does not include any leaves you could add a few sprigs of ivy.

1

2

4 Finally, add all the small pieces, like cherries or whatever your choice has been. Some of these have been left their original colour to add a spark of brilliance to the otherwise pastel collection. This bowl makes a stunning centrepiece for a buffet table or sideboard.

LEFT: This gorgeous whitewashed fruitbowl would be a major focal point for a party or gathering of family or friends.

Clematis Bookends

Unusual bookends such as these can be made with a few pieces of terracotta pottery, some lengths of wood and a little imagination. Other versions could also be created once friends and family have seen these and want different versions for themselves.

Flowers: *10 clematis flowers; 6 sprigs geranium leaves; a few curly twigs or tendrils.*
Equipment: *4 pieces wood, 15 cm (6 in) x 8 cm (3 in) x 2.5 cm (1 in) deep; 2 terracotta pots 10 cm (4 in), plus selection of miniature pots and jars; 1 block florist's foam.*

1 First glue the wood into two bases as shown in the photograph. Glue them securely so that they won't come adrift at some later date once your creation is finished! Once they are dry, using a hot glue gun, add the terracotta pots and jars in a random collection as shown in the example. It helps to place the two bookends in their final position so that you can point the largest flower pots in such a way that the flowers will be seen to their best advantage.

2 Fill the large pots with foam and place a small piece in one of the other smaller pots to take the secondary arrangement. Fill the large pot with some clematis leaves, making sure that the foam is completely covered once the flowers have been added. To the clematis foliage add a spray or two of the geranium leaves and a curly twig or tendril. Then place three clematis flowers into the foam. If the foam appears to be a little overcrowded, use your glue gun and glue the flowers into position.

3 Lastly, do the smaller arrangement. Make sure one of the smaller pots has a piece of foam wedged into it and repeat the last process. Place some clematis

Right: These clematis bookends are among the more unusual projects in the book but can be made very simply. They are extremely practical as they are quite heavy and hold books up very efficiently as well as looking lovely!

leaves into the foam, add a sprig of geranium leaves and a couple of clematis flowers. If you have any more tendrils, they can be added at this stage. Then stand back from the bookends and make sure that the balance is right and that none of the grey foam is visible.

Peony Firescreen

The joys of an open fire in the cold winter nights are not so obvious during the summer, when the gaping, and somewhat unattractive, hole looks very dull. With this dramatic firescreen you can use the opportunity to enjoy the magnificent form of the peony all summer long.

Flowers: *11 large peony flowers; 5 stems dark blue berries; 2 stems ivy.*
Equipment: *blockboard or similar base cut to fit the fireplace; 5 dark straw plaits (or more if your base is larger).*

Although I used my trusty hot glue gun again for this project, it could be made with a strong general adhesive if you were prepared to wait and hold the items as you fixed them.

1 The base board should be made from a fairly lightweight but rigid board, with two feet so that it stands securely, even with the weight of the flowers attached to it. Paint the finished board a suitable colour to match the decor of the room or the colours in the arrangement.

2 Attach the dark, twiggy plaits to the base board across the bottom and moving upwards. Fix them as firmly as you can as they are an important part of the design and other pieces will be attached to them. Where there is a small gap between the plaits, add a few ivy leaves here and there to give the effect of a rustic basket intertwined with ivy.

3 Gradually attach the foliage and flowers from the peonies. Some of the leaves can be cut from the stems and glued on individually to help cover the base board. Glue the stems as far up the board as possible to help them bear the weight of the flower head. It can be helpful to make the firescreen *in situ* so that you can see at a glance how high the flowers should be.

4 Finally, add the remaining peonies. Space them well so that the balance seems right. Do not have too many peonies on one side or the other, and have several coming fairly low down as though over the edge of the 'basket' formed by the plaits at the front. Then as a last touch glue in some sprays of berries to add interest to the arrangement. Small details can often make all the difference to both the depth and balance of the display. Your firescreen can now fill the fireplace for many summers, still looking as good as new after many years' service.

Right: The dilemma of what to fill the fireplace with in the summer can now be solved with an arrangement of beautiful peonies. Because it is mounted on a board screen, this project is not only easily moved for cleaning, it reduces the cost of the flowers dramatically as you need very few to achieve this effect.

Fabulous Floral Tiebacks

Once your collection of silk flowers and bits and pieces begins to grow you will soon accumulate some leftover items from previous projects you have made. An ideal way to use these up and produce some lovely focal points for a window is to make some floral or fruity tiebacks.

Flowers: *collection of approximately 15–20 flowers assorted but toning; 20 sprays leaves; 10 sprays buds, blossom or berries.*
Equipment: *pair of cord tiebacks; hooks to fix into the wall.*

RIGHT: This beautiful floral tieback is made on a standard cord base and can easily be made with flowers and foliage left over from other projects. It adds a unique touch to a pretty window.

LEFT: Parchment, rather than silk, roses have been used in this tieback. They are merely twisted around their own stems to make a circlet which slips around the curtain to hold it back, rather than being glued or permanently fixed.

1 Start with the foliage. This can be wound around the cord or fixed permanently with a little glue. I found a combination of both methods worked well. Bend the leaves and foliage around the wire and then add little touches of glue to fix them in position so that they do not slip once the tieback is in use.

2 Add some of the larger flowers. In this case they are pinky mauve orchids which add a lovely exotic touch to the design. Although the spray of orchids is fairly expensive, it breaks down into several flower heads and buds and goes quite a long way. It gives a better end result if the flowers are in co-ordinating colours rather than all twenty or so being completely different. The two tiebacks should look as similar as possible.

3 Fill the design with more large flowers and some of the smaller ones. Again, add touches of glue as well as twisting the wired stems around the cord. Try to make both ties at the same time so that they will be a fairly accurately matched pair. Making them one at a time makes it harder to match them.

4 Continue the garland of flowers along the cord until you have about a third left bare. This bare length will slip behind the curtain and remain unseen. Once the glue has dried you can fix the hooks into the wall and loop your tiebacks into position, then simply wait for the compliments! These floral ties can look as effective on plain curtains as on floral ones, but if they are going against floral fabric it is important to blend the colours carefully so that they co-ordinate.

RIGHT: This design is based on a solid brass tieback. The fruit is glued on with a hot glue gun, with the larger fruit going on first and the smaller pieces being added afterwards.

Orchid Chandelier

Such an amazing decoration obviously relies heavily on you having a suitable chandelier. However, other light fittings could be treated in a similar way, even if they do not achieve this quite magnificent end result.

Flowers: *3 strands vine leaves; 5-7 stems orchid flowers.*
Equipment: *1 chandelier (!)*

This is such a simple project that it hardly needs any instructions. One of the great advantages of artificial flowers is that they are almost all constructed with wires as an integral part of their stems. Therefore when you tackle a project that would normally require wiring fresh flowers, your work has already been done in advance and all your flowers are ready-wired!

1 Start with the plain chandelier (or any other light fitting) and wind the stems of vine leaves around some of the arms and up the centre of the fitting. How many leaves you use is partly a matter of personal choice and is also dependent upon the size of the chandelier. If your chandelier has only three arms you will need less foliage than a chandelier with seven or nine arms. The wired leaves should bend and twist nicely and stay in position. If you find they need a little help, you can either use a hot glue gun (the glue usually peels off later) or a little wire to fix them more firmly.

2 Once the leaves are in position the orchids can be added. These again will already be wired, which will make your job much easier. However, the flowers are usually not as pliable as stems or leaves so you may want to use some method of fixing, such as hot glue or wire, as mentioned in the previous paragraph.

If the candelabra that you are decorating holds candles rather than electric light bulbs, do take care not to leave it unattended whilst the candles are alight, as they would be a dangerous fire hazard. Even electric light bulbs touching artificial flowers could be a little unsafe as they can reach quite high temperatures, so do check and take care.

RIGHT: This beautiful chandelier decorated with orchids and vine leaves makes even an impromptu meal seem really special. You would only need ten minutes to attach the pieces to the chandelier frame – not long to create something special!

ROSY CANDELABRA

This pretty but simple idea is quick to make and only needs the minimum of materials. Of course, it could be made in any colour scheme to suit your tableware or a special occasion. The candelabra can also be painted and repainted to add a splash of colour to the basic theme and to suit the mood of the flowers you choose to use.

Flowers: *5 sprays scarlet briar roses with foliage.*
Equipment: *1 candelabra, metal or wooden, in your choice of colour scheme.*

Although it seems a little permanent, a hot glue gun is used in this project to attach the flowers and foliage to the candelabra. I usually find that with time and care you can peel all the glue, flowers and foliage off the candelabra when you want to change the arrangement.

1 Start with the foliage. The briar roses that I used were really simple to attach as every little leaf was wired and they were a pleasure to bend, twist and generally manipulate! Cut the foliage into single sprays of three or five leaves, depending on the variety that you have, and attach them to the candelabra starting at the base and climbing upwards in the same way that a rose would naturally climb. Having climbed up the stem of the candelabra, the leaves can then 'branch' out to the other sections of the item. Take care not to have any leaves too close to the candle holders as this may prevent the candles fitting or be a safety hazard once the candles are alight.

2 Glue on the rose heads. Trim the rose heads very close so that there is a minimal amount of stem. I usually find you can just pull and the heads slip off because of the way they are constructed. Then add the single rose heads to the candelabra, again starting at the base as this needs to have several blooms climbing around the central stem.

3 Scatter a few heads around the arms of the candelabra, trying to keep a balance so that there are an equal number of roses on either side. Again bear in mind the candles – the flowers should not get too close to them. The variety of rose used here had green rose buds which I scattered through the arrangement to add more detail and interest. You could also add extra touches such as a few sprays of gypsophila or some ribbons. Candles could be chosen in a matching colour, or in cream or ivory as a contrast.

RIGHT: This candelabra makes a very special focal point for a formal or informal occasion.

GILDING THE LILY

The strong and architectural form of the lily is wonderfully highlighted in this dramatic table centrepiece using a range of metallic paints. Complement the arrangement with tall candles in bold colours.

Flowers: *5 strands vine; 7 large lilies with buds; scraps of other leaves and berries for napkins.*
Equipment: *30 cm (12 in) diameter florist's foam ring; 6 candles; 6 candle holders – or wires (optional); gold, silver, bronze, copper and pewter effect paint.*

The first and most laborious task of this project is to paint all the ingredients. You can use all the paints specified or just a few of them. The flowers and foliage in the example here were painted with combinations of six different colours. The golden items were painted with bright gold and then streaked with antique gold. The silver pieces were painted silver and then streaked with pewter. The coppery items were painted with copper and streaked with bronze. The candles were also streaked with gold and silver paint.

1 Once the paint has completely dried, the first step is to place some stems of the painted vine around the foam ring. Make sure that the stem is well embedded in the foam and then catch other pieces of the stem with the occasional hairpin made from stub wire. If you wish to use candle holders then it is sensible to place them in the arrangement now while there is still plenty of room to manoeuvre. Alternatively, the candles can have small hairpins of wire taped around the bases to act as feet to steady them.

ABOVE: This very impressive formal setting is a relatively simple arrangement in stunning gilded and silvery colours.

LEFT: Twist some foliage into a circle and add a few berries by twining them around the stems – hey presto, instant napkin rings!

2 Next, fill the ring more thoroughly with trailing pieces of vine. Where they will not stay in place use more wire hair pins. Try to mix the different colours for the best result.

3 Add the lilies into the arrangement. Separate the large flowers from the buds and place them individually, so that you can control where they are going in order to add the greatest impact. Make sure the open lilies are towards the outside of the arrangement so that they are most visible to your dinner guests.

4 Finally, place the candles into position and fill any gaps with odd leaves or bits and pieces to make sure that none of the foam is visible. Do remember never to leave candles burning when you leave the table as they are a fire hazard.

Rose Garden Lamp

Inspired by Victorian style, this project combines some really pretty, feminine full-blown roses with lace, touches of blossom and some lovely deep green rose leaves. Ideal as an accessory for a truly feminine boudoir, this glamorous lamp would make a wonderful gift for a close friend or a treat for yourself.

Flowers: *11 very large old fashioned roses; 3 stems cream blossom.*
Equipment: *plain lamp base and shade; 3–4 m (3–4 yds) of 2.5–5 cm (1–2 in) wide lace (depending upon how lavish you want your design to be).*

The hot glue gun comes into its own again here. It makes this project so simple. Without such a gadget it would be very lengthy and tiresome, waiting for glue to dry as you attached each component piece.

1 Start to outline your design with the foliage as this gives you an idea of where you want the bulk of the decoration to be. Try not to over decorate the shade and then leave the base completely bare, as this makes it seem very top heavy. Cut off the leaves individually or in sprays of three, depending upon the size of the foliage that accompanies your roses. Again, this particular variety of rose was fully wired so it was very easy to twist the leaves around the base in the direction required.

2 Make a lace bow with reasonably long streamers and attach this to the base of the lamp. Then cut the remaining lace into lengths approximately 15 cm (6 in) long and make into double loops; twist a little wire around the base of the loops to hold them in position. Attach these loops on to the spiralling rose leaves, placing them in such a way that the roses, when they are finally added, will cover the wire binding.

3 Carefully attach the large roses. These should spiral across the shade and form a group at the base of the shade. Place them so that each one is clearly visible and does not squash another. Make sure that the lace is also easily seen rather than caught under or hidden beneath a flower.

4 Lastly, add small clusters of cream blossom for an extra dainty touch to the design. This lends a more filigree air to the sprays of flowers and the whole lamp looks wonderfully feminine.

RIGHT: *This beautiful lamp would look gorgeous on a bedside table or near a dressing table in a lady's bedroom, or perhaps in a floral guest room.*

Wall Flowers

So many of us are limited for space nowadays with more compact housing and more possessions to fit in! Flowers can be especially effective on the walls as they are raised up and therefore become far more visible. There are many unusual ideas in this section which will hopefully set your mind thinking along new lines and inspire you to create some masterpieces using the wide selection of silk flowers, fruit and foliage available.

KITCHEN WALL HANGING

Miniature fruit and vegetables are a delight to work with. Combine your collection with small bread rolls and leaves to make a witty decoration for the kitchen.

Flowers and food: *8 bread rolls dried and varnished – or made from salt dough; 1 small spray red/brown vine leaves; 2 stems cotoneaster berries; selection of small vegetables including aubergines, pumpkins, sweetcorn and peaches.*
Equipment: *1 bread or chopping board, round or rectangular.*

The ingredients are all attached using a hot glue gun. If you want to use an ordinary adhesive, do allow enough time for each piece to dry before you add the next item – in some cases it will take up to 24 hours to dry, as building one piece on to another that is not secure will result in your decoration on the floor!

RIGHT: This attractive miscellany of vegetables and berries looks wonderful against the wooden board and would grace any kitchen. It could also make an interesting gift for a keen cook!

1 Begin with some leaves to soften the edges of the board and also the arrangement. You do not need to use many as you do not want to obscure the wood of the board. However, if you are using an old chopping board that is not in pristine condition, you might want to obscure quite a lot of the board! Place some of the bread rolls in position to fill the space in the centre of the board.

2 Build up the design by adding the rest of the bread rolls and some of the vegetables. This takes a certain amount of trial and error as certain shapes may look better in one position than another.

3 Continue glueing on the vegetables until you are happy that the board is full enough. Make sure that you do not end up adding gratuitous pieces of vegetable just because you have them in front of you. It is very tempting to carry on adding bits and pieces because you are enjoying yourself. Every piece on the board should be visible and not be buried under a mountain of other elements.

4 Finally, snip the berries into small pieces with a little stem and glue them around the edges of the arrangement and through the middle just to soften the lines

a little and add some extra detail. The finished arrangement can be sprayed with aerosol varnish if you wish to help preserve it, and it is slightly easier to dust if it has been varnished although this is not essential.

Garland of Delphiniums

Pink roses blend with blue and cream delphiniums and an assortment of vine leaves to make a particularly pretty combination. This abundant collection falls beautifully over the pine corner cupboard but could grace many other pieces of furniture.

Equipment: *thick cord cut to the required length, plus about 15 cm (6 in) for loops; 1 m (1 yd) 5 cm (2 in) wide ribbon; 1m (yd) 2.5 cm (1 in) wide ribbon; a few florist's stub wires.*
Flowers: *5 stems blue delphiniums: 5 stems cream or white delphiniums; 18–20 roses and foliage.*

1 Begin by turning over the ends of the cord and binding them to make hanging loops. If it is to drape, as in the photograph here, then you will only need a wire loop in the middle behind the bow; the other fixings can be organized later. If, however, it is to be strung across a dresser or door then the loops are essential.

Make two bows from the ribbons (see page 13) and wire or glue them into position in the middle of the cord. The larger bow is naturally fixed on first, and then the second placed in the centre. The vine can then be twined around the cord. As all the leaves and the stems are already wired, you should be able to achieve this without needing any stub wires, but if you are having difficulty then use some extra wire as well.

2 The delphiniums will have to be cut down before they are added into the garland as they are usually very long. By cutting the stems carefully you should be able to use every one of the flowers. These should be wired in to the garland; bind them tightly on to the cord with some florist's wire. Although they are already wired, the stems are very stiff and will not be easily bent.

3 Wire in the cream delphiniums in the same manner, spacing them equally so that there is a balance in the colours along the entire length.

4 The roses can be pulled off their stems and glued into position, winding along the full length with an equal number on each side of the bows.

RIGHT: The shower of summer flowers adds such a lovely touch to the pine cabinet. The same treatment can work wonders for dull bookcases, dressers or even doorways.

Woodland Mirror

This delightful fantasy mirror is another of my favourite projects in this book. The mirror and hardboard base are easily constructed and after that it depends on your flights of fancy as to how the mirror turns out.

Plants and birds: *selection of leaves and foliage including some ivy; 2 pieces artificial twig; 7–9 stems assorted wild or woodland flowers; small bunch of artificial toadstools; 2 small birds.*
Equipment: *oval piece of mirror glass approximately 35 cm (14 in) x 30 cm (12 in); oval piece of hardboard 45 cm (18 in) x 4 cm (16 in) with hanger attached.*

Fixing the mirror glass to the oval hardboard back is very important. This must be done securely as the whole of the project rests on this point. There are several brands of strong bonding adhesive available. You could resort to the hot glue gun but I feel a stronger adhesive would be advisable. Make sure the mirror is placed centrally on the hardboard so that you have plenty of room all round the mirror to stick the flowers and foliage. Make sure there is a strong D-ring hanger or similar fitment attached to the back of the hardboard before you glue the mirror glass on to it.

1 Start by fixing a garland of leaves around the outside of the mirror. Mix several different varieties of leaf, choosing some that are dark and glossy and others that will contrast in both colour and shape. It is important to cover all the brown hardboard with leaves to avoid the backing board showing through.

2 Fix on an artificial twig or two; bend and twist them to add interest to the design. The ivy is attached to the top of the mirror so that it can cascade down the left hand side.

3 Finally, you can add the flowers in small natural groups as though they were growing. Although you do not want to obscure the mirror too much, it does look effective if some of the larger flowers are reflected in the glass, creating an interesting double image. Tuck small groups of toadstools around the base. Take care to place things in positions that are as natural as possible – a bird perched on a twig perhaps and a cluster of toadstools nestled amongst the leaves.

Right: This delightful mirror creates a very special focal point. The wild woodland feel is created by using artificial twigs, mushrooms and tiny birds.

Wooden Harvest Frame

Here is an unusual picture frame that looks like a wood carving, perhaps in the style of Grinling Gibbons. It is created from small scented wooden fruit, which are gradually built up on a plain wooden frame. If you would prefer a darker colour, the entire frame with fruit could then be stained or coloured once the frame is complete.

Fruit and flowers: *selection of wooden fruit and flowers.*
Equipment: *plain wooden picture frame with a 30 cm (12 in) x 25 cm (10 in) aperture and flat, wide moulding; stain or paint if required.*

If wooden fruits are not available in your area then other artificial fruits or flowers could be used instead.

1

2

3

Right: Create this stylish frame by collecting small wooden fruit and glueing them on to a plain pine or wooden frame. The hot glue gun comes into its own again, but other strong adhesives could be used instead.

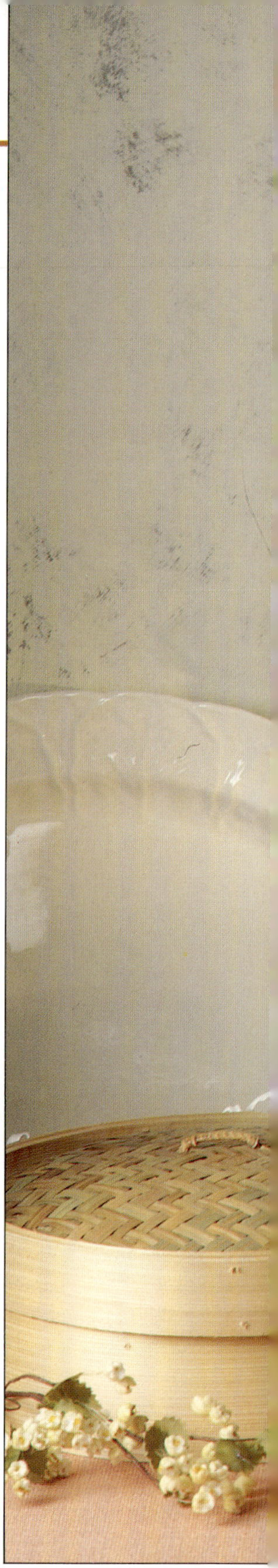

1 The frame should be clean and free from grease to give a secure base on which to glue the items. The design should be built up, starting with some larger fruits to help fill the space on the frame, with smaller fruits following to fill the gaps. The star fruit pictured in the first stage of the project were simple to attach to the frame as they have flattened ribs. Use plenty of glue to make sure they are firmly stuck on, but do not dribble the glue over the fruit or frame, otherwise it will be visible on the completed project.

2 Gradually build up each side of the frame, filling the bigger spaces with single fruit and tiny gaps with smaller pieces. Take care that each piece is firmly fixed before attaching the next fruit.

3 Once you are happy with the frame you can either spray it with aerosol varnish, paint it with a straightforward matte or gloss varnish (much more time consuming than spraying it!). You could stain the entire project with a wood stain, although you will find that household ingredients from the kitchen can be just as useful as wood stains. I have often used dark soy sauce as a wood stain or to age something rather rapidly!

This could also be made as a mirror frame or to hold photographs, depending on which you would prefer. It does look particularly striking as a mirror frame as there is no image to detract from the complex structure around the frame.

Ring of Hydrangeas

Hydrangeas, roses and gypsophila decorate a willow ring with the addition of some beautiful cream silk, wired-edge ribbon. Often special ribbons can make or break a design, and can lift an arrangement from the mundane to the absolutely wonderful.

Flowers: *5 heads hydrangea in assorted colours; 5 large roses; 1 large spray gypsophila.*
Equipment: *2 m (2 yds) ribbon 5–8 cm (2–3 in) wide preferably wired at the edges; 23–25 cm (9–10 in) willow ring.*

Wreaths have always provided a traditional way of decorating walls, doors and entrances. It is an attractive way of welcoming friends and guests to your home. This summery design uses a relatively new development in silk flowers, those intended to look similar to dried flowers.

1 It is essential to place the bow in position first to make sure that it is well fixed on to the willow ring. A hot glue gun is excellent for this purpose. Given some pressure on the bow and plenty of glue,

RIGHT: This pretty ring would be an ideal bathroom or bedroom decoration with the gorgeous cream ribbon adding a touch of luxury. The soft shades of pinks and blues are gentle enough to mix with many other colour schemes.

LEFT: This little fairy ring has a much daintier feel and is reminiscent of a fantasy woodland. The tiny toadstools look very realistic and make a pretty focal point.

the bow is fixed very securely (so much so you may not be able to change your mind and move it!). Make two bows in the manner described on page 13. Use wire-edged ribbon to make them twist and curve in an attractive way. Make one bow slightly larger than the other and glue that into position first, and then add the smaller of the two bows into the centre.

2 Using the leaves that are provided with the hydrangea heads, separate them from the flowers and glue them on to the ring on either side of the ribbons as shown in the photograph.

3 Place the hydrangea heads in and around the ribbons and around one half of the ring. If necessary the heads can be dismantled and used as several smaller pieces as this is the way that the hydrangea is constructed.

4 Glue in the roses, making sure that they are fairly prominent as they are an important feature of the design. Finally, add some sprays of gypsophila to lighten the arrangement and add a little delicacy to the edges of the ring.

Silk Magnolias

This modern minimal arrangement shows how beautiful some silk flowers can be. Now that the manufacturers have taken so many leaps forward in improving artificial flowers, magnolias have become prized specimens that can be displayed on their own as illustrated here.

Flowers: *5 magnolias with buds; moss to cover the hardboard.*

Equipment: *20 cm (8 in) x 15 cm (6 in) piece of hardboard with hanging ring.*

There is some artifice in constructing even the most simple of displays, as demonstrated by this elegant wall-hanging. The flowers have been glued on with only relatively short stems and the other part of the stem is attached separately. Do ensure that the hanging mechanism is attached to the hardboard before you start glueing on the flowers, as this is a tricky operation, and one that is nearly impossible once the arrangement is finished.

1 Place the hardboard with the hanger underneath and trim a couple of magnolias to about 12 cm (5 in) in length. Carefully keep the other half of the stem, bend it to make the lines appear more interesting and glue it securely on to the board as well.

2 Continue glueing the flowers and buds on to the board in the same way and then add the stems at the base of the design, so that you create an attractive representation of a bunch of magnolias.

LEFT: An unusual and lovely bunch of silk magnolia flowers makes a dramatic decoration that would look perfect in a number of rooms: bathroom, bedroom or living room.

3 There will be bare areas of board that are not covered and these should be covered with a little glue and some moss of any variety. The same techniques could be used with many different varieties of silk flowers or foliage. A huge bunch of peonies or full blown roses would look glorious with a corresponding number of stems. Take care that there are always enough stems to balance the flowers.

AUTUMN GATHERING

The golden colours of autumn are some compensation for the ending of summer, although they too fade away all too quickly. This simple wallhanging makes the most of attractive foliage reproduced in all its glory in silk form. The copper beech sprays can, of course, be substituted with any other leaf you find available.

Flowers: *7–9 sprays copper beech leaves; 5 sprays honesty pods; 3 sprays Chinese lanterns; 1 stem artificial twigs; assorted berries and hops.*
Equipment: *1 piece hardboard 20 cm (8 in) x 15 cm (6 in) with a D-ring or other hanger attached.*

Do make sure that a hanger has been firmly attached to the back of the hardboard before you make a start on your creation, as it is extremely difficult to provide a means of hanging it once you have finished. Also do make sure that you have the hanger in the correct position.

1 If necessary, trim the copper beech into sprays no more than 15 cm (6 in) long to prevent the plaque becoming unwieldy. Attach longer sprays to each end of the hardboard to give an elongated shape and fill in with other smaller sprays to achieve something approximating the shape shown in the photograph. This provides your base.

2 Twist and add in the stem of artificial twigs; they add interesting texture and detail to the arrangement. Then glue in some honesty pods and the Chinese lanterns. The glowing orange of these little lanterns adds a splash of colour. As they are silk the colour will last for many years and they will not drop or break, unlike their dried counterparts.

3 Fill the middle of the arrangement with a selection of berry sprays. Try to have a variation in size. Here I have used rose hips, smaller cotoneaster berries, snow berries and sloes in the selection.

4 Finally, add a generous twist of hops across the twigs in the centre to give a stronger focal point, and add any further berries that you feel may be necessary.

LEFT: This unusual wall decoration is a wonderful reminder of autumn walks in the woods, and can also be a lovely way to use oddments that would otherwise linger in the box of spare bits and pieces!

Sunflower Bulletin Board

Bring a ray of brilliant sunshine into an office, study, or kitchen with this bright and sunny notice board. It is an easy project, particularly if you use a hot glue gun, and apart from making up the baseboard it should only take you a short while with no more than a handful of flowers.

Flowers: *3 large sunflowers; 3 wild artichokes; 2 sprays green eucalyptus; 12 chamomile daisy heads.*

Equipment: *a piece of fibreboard or other suitable soft board that will take drawing pins easily (do ensure that a hanger is fixed to the back); paint; ribbon.*

Making up the baseboard is by far the most complicated part of this project, so if you have friends nearby who enjoy such challenges then share this project with them! You could use a straight rectangular board if you do not fancy cutting out the curves with a jigsaw. Once you have created a board the shape that you want, paint it with at least two coats of emulsion paint in matt or silk finish. Something bright like this pale yellow looks stunning and is likely to be well covered by notes and jottings so may not be as dominant as it at first appears.

1 Once the paint is completely dry, lay some ribbon across the board to make the trellis pattern as illustrated in the photograph. The ribbons can be stretched around the back of the board and attached with drawing pins, staples or even glue. I found drawing pins a fairly simple way as they can be pressed in by feel without having to turn the board around. The daisies have just been glued on as a decoration; they are only glued to the ribbon and not to the board, so letters can still slip down behind them.

2 To decorate the top portion, first add some sprigs of greenery, in this case eucalyptus, then firmly glue three large sunflowers to the centre. I have attached them slightly off centre to balance the wild artichokes that are added next.

3 Once the sunflowers and the eucalyptus are in position, trim the stalks off the wild artichokes and stick the heads into the arrangement. The display could be further embellished with some more greenery or another component but the beautiful sunflowers are probably best left to shine on their own.

2

1

3

RIGHT: This is an enjoyable project to make up. It is very useful, and looks fabulous. The bright yellow is such a happy colour and just a touch of it is enough to make a corner of the room sparkle.

RAG DOLLS AND DAISIES

Children and adults will not be able to resist this charming garland for the nursery. It combines pretty rag dolls with practical silk flowers and foliage that can be washed or wiped to keep them dust free.

Flowers: *curved bundle of twigs – see text; 5–7 sprays geranium leaves; 5 large sprays green eucalyptus leaves; 6 pieces chamomile daisy spray.*
Equipment: *ribbon to match the room or the dolls; 4 small rag dolls.*

The curved bundle of twigs was bought already made up from a craft shop. However, if you can't find anything similar, you could make one from twigs and sticks from the garden and tie them with wire and raffia.

1 Start with the eucalyptus. This is usually sold in quite long sprays, so cut it down into sprigs of a more manageable length. These should be spread along the curve to form a base on which to add the other items. Other foliage would also be suitable as long as it is a fresh green tone to blend with the light, bright colouring of the daisy flowers.

2 Add the geranium leaves. These leaves are particularly attractive as they are variegated and the cream tinges on the leaves brighten the arrangement and look very pretty. You could use double quantity of the first foliage if you don't want to buy a second variety, but it does add extra interest to the finished garland. Tie three bows either in a traditional shoelace manner or by the method described on page 13. Choose a light-hearted ribbon like this pink gingham that will add to the overall appeal to young children of this decoration.

3 Fix the dolls in position. Just apply a good amount of glue to their backs (without flinching!) and press them securely on to the garland. Miniature teddies, scarecrows, even small soft toys could also be used for this charming and delightful nursery decoration.

LEFT: This enchanting child's decoration can be hung safely out of the way of small hands to stop them dismantling it while your back is turned.

ABOVE: A box of sweet rag dolls was found by chance, but many other alternatives are possible, such as teddies or cats.

4 Finish the garland by snipping the sprays of daisy into small pieces, perhaps two or three flowers together, and glue them into the foliage. Choosing daisies gives this a lovely young-at-heart feel, however you could adapt it with any other flower that took your fancy.

FESTIVE FLAIR

Celebrations and special occasions are the most marvellous excuse to let your imagination run riot with weddings, family occasions and special anniversaries all lending themselves to wonderful floral extravaganzas. Silk and parchment flowers and artificial fruit come into their own here as they can be prepared well in advance, leaving you to enjoy the festivities.

Festive Fireplace

There is an amazing range of silk flowers and other accessories that could be included in a Christmas design such as this, but I chose to avoid flowers completely and used some gilded grapes, cherubs and masses of velvet ribbon and gold leaves.

Plants and models: *artificial spruce or fir garland; 8 bunches of dark purple grapes; 5 small plaster cherubs; assortment of green leaves in small sprays.*
Equipment: *1.5 m (1½ yds) green velvet ribbon; 1.5 m (1½ yds) red velvet ribbon.*

This is such a gorgeous decoration that it is well worth the little time that it takes to make it. The best bit of news is that the garland comes ready made. You will need to prepare the cherubs and grapes and the gold leaves. The cherubs were first painted with a coat of Venetian red acrylic paint and, once they were dry, a badly applied coat of antique gold paint was painted on top. Try to leave patches unpainted so that the red shows through. The leaves can be hand painted or sprayed with gold, and the grapes touched up with gold paint here and there, allowing plenty of the purple colouring to show through.

1 The ribbons should be made into bows using the method described and illustrated on page 13, and then glued to the centre of the garland. I have attached the green bows to the left of centre and the red slightly right of centre but you could arrange them differently.

2 Once the cherubs are dry they can also be glued into position. Use plenty of glue and make sure that they are not balancing perilously on a single pine needle. I have placed one in the centre and the other four equally spaced two each side of the garland.

3 Next, attach the bunches of grapes, again placing equal numbers each side of the ribbons, so in this case there are four each side. You could use more or less depending upon your budget.

4 Finally glue in the small sprays of gilded leaves right across the garland to add golden highlights across the fireplace. You can add other golden accessories, such as apples, if you wish.

RIGHT: This glamorous garland would really steal the show at Christmas. Being made from artificial ingredients it can also be carefully stored away and brought out again the following year!

Christmas Stocking

Hanging up a stocking for Santa is a very enjoyable tradition for all ages! The basic stocking can be made at home or you can buy a plain felt one in red or green from most craft stores or fabric departments. This stocking was made from red velvet and then trimmed with some old lace. Remember to add a hanging loop!

Leaves and fruit: *1 spray orange/red vine leaves; assorted fruit including plums and cherries; some ivy leaves and smaller pieces of fruit.*
Equipment: *1 Christmas stocking.*

1 First firmly attach the vine leaves individually to the top right-hand corner of the stocking. Alternatively if the spray is the right size and shape this could be glued straight on to the stocking, but usually the vine sprays are too spaced out and the gaps too large for this project. Use some of the tendrils as well to add interest to the design.

2 Next glue on the larger items in a fairly tight group in the centre of the leaves, fitting them together as best you can. Other varieties of fruit can be used,

RIGHT: A cornucopia of fruit cascading down the stocking adds to the Christmas feeling of abundance and celebration.

or fruit that has been sprayed gold is another option.

3 Fill in the arrangement with small ivy leaves and tiny pieces of fruit and vine tendrils, so that the red of the stocking does not show through the fruit.

There are a host of other possibilities for decorating a Christmas stocking for other members of the family. The children could have toys or sweets, bricks or animals attached in the same way, with a backing of leaves perhaps to soften the group. Father's stocking could have miniature gardening tools or pots, fishing flies or items relating to his hobby. Even the pets could be given a stocking with catnip mice and other toys, or bones and biscuits tied with ribbons for the dog. The only limit is your imagination!

ADORABLE CHERUB WREATH

Delightful cherubs made of plaster caught my eye when I found them in an accessories catalogue. They make the perfect accompaniment to the unusual blue-toned poinsettias, adding to the stunning effect of the wreath. Again, because this decoration is made from silk flowers, it can be put away and brought out Christmas after Christmas.

Flowers and models: *5 blue/grey poinsettias; 3 plaster cherubs or angels.*
Equipment: *dark blue, gold and silver paint; a little gold cord; straw ring approximately 30 cm (12 in) diameter*

First you must paint the cherubs or angels. Coat them all over with some dark blue paint; it looks a little strange but is, after all, only the undercoat! Once the blue paint is dry then roughly cover with silver paint, allowing some of the blue to show through. Then as a final touch, streak some antique gold paint over some of the silver. This gives a lovely antique effect and tones beautifully with the poinsettias.

1 Leave three of the poinsettias whole, but dismantle the other two into smaller groups of petals. Glue some of the petals around the straw ring to create a base on which to place the cherubs.

1

RIGHT: This is another of my favourite projects from this book. A wreath such as this can be treasured from one year to the next and brought out to shouts of 'Oh do you remember that?'. Silk flowers definitely win on many counts!

2

3

2 Once the cherubs are completely dry, glue them on really firmly with some poinsettia petals around them. Make sure that they are well stuck on to the wreath as they are quite heavy. If you cannot buy plaster cherubs then other Christmas motifs might work instead. There are often angels, cherubs or fairies amongst the Christmas tree decorations that might make a good substitute.

3 Finally, glue on the three whole poinsettias between the cherubs and use up the rest of the single or double petals to fill out the circle. Add some loops of gold cord to give that finishing touch.

LILIES FOR THE BRIDE

Romantic, filmy net fabric with tiny dots is here intertwined with sumptuous lilies to make an unusual bouquet to complement the bride in white. As it is silk, the bouquet could be made many weeks or months ahead provided that it is kept clean and dust free.

Flowers: *7 large white lilies with buds.*
Equipment: *1 m (1 yd) soft net with dots or other tiny motifs; ivory wire-edged ribbon; florist's stub wires.*

1 Cut the net into narrow strips about 10–15 cm (4–6 in) wide. Bend the strip into a long loop and bind it with a little wire. Attach a net loop to every stem of lily so that the net comes up near the flower. This will help to give a feeling of fullness and abundance to the bouquet.

2 Lay the lilies out very carefully on a flat surface and place one slightly higher, then a couple a little lower down. Arrange the netting and, if necessary, bend the flowers to look as balanced and attractive as possible.

3 Once you have all the lilies laid into a bunch, take some stub wire and very firmly wire the bunch together in one spot. If necessary use two or three wires until you are really happy that the bunch is secure. Then attach the wide ribbon and tie into a bow. As the ribbon is wire-edged it will bend into whatever shape you want. The bouquet can now be gently bent and manipulated to move any flowers into gaps or spaces that worry you until you feel that the balance is perfect.

If you plan a wedding with silk flowers, the main bonus is the extra time that you have. When you are making up fresh flowers everything is always a last minute panic with all the arrangements, head-dresses and bouquets having to be made the day before or worse still the night before! With silk flowers, however, you can make things at your leisure.

1

RIGHT: A tied bunch of lilies is not difficult to create and would look wonderful with many styles of wedding dress. A similar technique could also be used with roses or any other special flowers.

2

Romantic Head-dress

Here is a spectacular head-dress for a bride looking for something more unusual and that retains the romance of red roses. With silk flowers there is the special plus that the head-dress can be kept for ever in tissue in the drawer for you to admire on a rainy day and bring back happy memories.

Flowers: *5 large red roses; a few ivy leaves; 5 sprays sloe berries; 7 large red rose hips; 7–10 pieces bear grass.*
Equipment: *1 wide non-slip hair band*

This entire project is made with the help of a hot glue gun. There is an additional bonus to the usual ones of speed and ease in this case, as decorations worn on the head must be safe – wired items can cause nasty scratches unless they are wired very professionally – and with a glue gun you have no such worries.

1 Use a good quality wide hair band. This one was made from green velvet with a non-slip band underneath. If you buy a solid plastic band they can be a little slippery. Where the leaves are already wired, you can wind the wire around the hair band and glue the leaves as well for extra security. It is wise to remember throughout this project that the head-dress will be worn on a very important occasion so check and double check that everything is securely fixed and will not slip!

2 Firmly glue on all the roses, and then add some of the rose foliage all the way round the band. Make sure the roses look right when the head-dress is being worn. If you have a model head then this makes the job a great deal easier – the normal alternative is to try the head-dress on whilst looking in a mirror. Some more ivy leaves will help fill some gaps.

3 Cut the berries into small sprigs. If you leave them too long and glue them into the head-dress they will look very much like antennae which might not be exactly what the bride wanted. Place the berries all along the band and then glue in some individual rose hips at intervals between the roses.

4 Make the lengths of bear grass into small double loops and bind with a little silver rose wire or fuse wire. Glue these loops in throughout the design to give a little extra dainty detail.

LEFT: A romantic head-dress is simple to make at home, and being silk it can be kept as a memento of your day.

MAGICAL SILVER WEDDING RING

Wild roses and silver net fabric make a beautiful present for a couple celebrating their silver wedding anniversary, and will serve long after to remind them of the occasion. The colour scheme could also be converted very simply to a golden version for a fiftieth anniversary, to a Christmas ring or an everyday wreath with colours to tone with your hallway or bedroom.

Equipment: *willow or twig ring 35 cm (14 in) diameter; 2 m (2 yds) silvery netting.*
Flowers: *3 stems ivy; 5 sprays berries; 3–4 stems pale blue larkspur; 7 sprays white wild roses; 5 sprays cream/yellow blossom.*

The addition of silver fabric to this ring changes it from something ordinary to something quite spectacular. If you find it difficult to buy silver netting, you could try using silver lamé or other silvery fabric. As a final resort you could try spraying white net with silver aerosol paint. It is not excellent but is better than no fabric at all!

1 Trim two wide strips, about 20 cm (8 in) or so from the length of fabric. Make these into bows using the method described and illustrated in the introduction. Then take the length of fabric left over and twine it around the ring. Glue one end with some glue from the hot glue gun and hold it while the glue sets (only a minute or so). Then fix the other end down so that the fabric cannot slip. If necessary add a few dots of glue on other points of the circle to keep the fabric in place.

2 Glue on the trailing pieces of ivy. Place some glue on the end of the stem of ivy and push it into the ring, then add further glue where necessary to make the ivy trail where you want it to. Concentrate mainly on the gaps between the silver fabric. Then add some clumps of sloe berries, making sure they are not too long.

3 Next add some white roses and the blue larkspur into the groups of flowers. In the example here I have kept the bow slightly off centre but you could have the bow full centre or off to the right.

4 Finally, add some white roses to the area around the bow and some small sprigs of creamy yellow blossom – these are, in fact, a fantasy flower but they are very pretty and add a little splash of colour to the ring.

1

2

3

4

RIGHT: *The ethereal quality of this silvery wreath is simple to achieve with the minimum of material. It is a flexible design that can easily be altered to gold or ruby for other anniversaries.*

ROSES FOR A GOLDEN WEDDING

A golden wedding is truly an occasion to celebrate. This cake is a special floral tribute but is still simple enough for anyone to tackle and does not present the pitfalls of arranging fresh flowers or require the skill needed for sugar flowers or complicated cake icing.

Flowers: *a selection of cream, yellow and rust roses; green rose foliage; a few green and cream orchids.*
Equipment: *silk ribbon: flower picks available from sugarcraft shops (see text).*

If you are making a smaller version of this, or just decorating the cake at home for a small party, you may like to lay the flowers on the cake without fixing them. However, if you want to fix them into the cake it is probably best to visit a sugarcraft shop. There is a new gadget available to push the stems of the flowers into before inserting them into the cake.

1 Start by making up a double bow in some ribbon in a matching colour to the cake. Wire it firmly around the middle and leave a length of wire to place into the flower pick which is pressed into the cake at whatever point you like.

2 Carefully place each flower stem into a flower pick, or in the case of the little cluster on the top of the cake, all the stems can be grouped together and placed in the pick and then pushed into the cake.

3 Start from the top and work downwards, using the larger roses on the bottom tiers so that they are not top heavy. If you are unsure where you want to put everything, balance it in position first before pushing anything through the icing and making a permanent mark.

The boards used on the base are much larger than usual, as this helps to balance the flowers. Although the finished result looks difficult to copy it is fairly simple, although it might be worth practising with smaller versions before committing yourself to something so large.

RIGHT: Roses and orchids, favourite floral gifts on such occasions, are used here to create a magical feeling of nostalgia and romance. They are a fitting tribute to a lifetime of happiness together.

NATURAL GIFTWRAP

Wrapping presents is always time consuming, but given a small stock of silk flowers and fruits, really impressive presentations can be achieved in a matter of minutes. The expense begins to recede once you have been arranging silk flowers for a while and have some scraps that look wonderful but will have cost you very little.

Flowers: *2 pansies.*
Equipment: *interesting handmade or rough paper; several lengths gardener's string.*

The basic principles of using artificial flowers as giftwrap are set out opposite using only one possible combination, but many others, that are just as simple, are possible.

FAR RIGHT: This lovely collection of parcels takes only the tiniest amount of flowers but looks very exciting. The parcel at the back has a piece of twig and some acorns, the one in the foreground is decorated with hops.

1 First, carefully wrap the parcel. If you are wrapping something that is an awkward shape, placing it in a box first is often the quickest way to ensure a perfectly professional finish to the corners! Take several strands of string – in this case about a dozen – and twist them together. Then use them to tie around the parcel in a traditional manner.

2 Finally use two large pansy flowers and either just tuck them through the knot or use some glue to hold them in position. Many combinations of fruit and flowers are possible and can be suited to the occasion. Combine with small objects such as candles to make an extra present that also looks attractive.

LEFT AND RIGHT: The pretty combinations of floral giftwrap decoration are endless. Combine artificial fruit or flowers with ribbons, cord or string and delight the recepient with your originality and thoughtfulness.

FLORAL GIFTS

Few people are impervious to the charm of a gift of flowers, but who does not regret that a floral bouquet or basket will fade away within a few days. For those times when you would like your gift to be more permanent, but still want to convey the unspoken messages of flowers, artificial fruits and flowers can provide a surprisingly imaginative answer. Try a few of the ideas shown here on your friends and see how well they are received!

BASKETS OF FLOWERS

When you are given a bouquet it is sometimes difficult to know what to do with it. But an arrangement that is already in a basket, and that can be displayed as it is, can be much more welcome.

Flowers: *10 large stems eucalyptus foliage; 5 stems blue larkspur; 5 mauve chrysanthemums; 7 pale pink scabious; 9 stems pale pink/mauve orchid.*
Equipment: *pink pastel basket; 1 block florist's foam; 1 small plastic frog attachment for the florist's foam.*

All the pastel baskets used in these projects have been coloured by spraying them with car spray paint or florist's spray. They were all pale white willow to begin with. Coloured baskets make a pleasant change, attractive though pale and dark stained baskets can be. You also have a much wider range of colours to complement your flowers once you start to use painted baskets.

1 Glue the frog attachment into the base of the basket. Push the foam down on to the prongs of the frog in order to keep it in position. Place the greenery into the arrangement, taking care not to go higher than the handle. There is no point in having a handle on the basket if you completely cover it up! Come out longer at the sides to add an attractive flowing shape to the basket.

2 Add the long stems of larkspur, trimmed if necessary, to the top and sides of the arrangement. The chrysanthemums should go in next while there is still plenty of room. Make sure they are longer than the foliage, but not by too much.

3 Finally, add the scabious and the orchids. The orchids should be placed to the sides so that they trail beautifully over the edges of the arrangement to soften it.

ABOVE: This trio can be displayed together or as individual baskets, as the colours complement each other but each is strong enough to stand on its own.

ABOVE: Although silk flowers can be expensive, think of how many years' pleasure they could give in comparison with the relatively short period that fresh flowers last.

RIGHT: Sweet peas are one of the most beautiful summer flowers but they do not last a long time either in the garden or cut in arrangements indoors. This arrangement will go on for ever!

A Bouquet of Carnations

This dazzling bouquet looks wonderful when presented as an ordinary bunch of flowers, but if you can wrap them in a suitable piece of fabric it can be converted into a permanent arrangement.

Flowers: *6–7 stems copper red foliage; 12 blooms in toning pinks, mainly carnations and roses; 3 sprays gypsophila-style blossom.*
Equipment: *large square of forest green silk or satin; 2 m (2 yds) green ribbon; 1 block florist's foam.*

1 Place the block of foam in the middle of the piece of fabric which needs to be about 60 cm (24 in) square. Arrange the foliage in the middle of the block, taking care to keep the leaves in the uppermost part of the block, rather than letting them go in at the sides.

2 Add all the major flowers, again sticking them all in the top side of the foam as the material added later will cover the sides.

3 Push in sprigs of the gypsophila-inspired blossom between the larger blooms to act as a contrast and to add some pretty details.

4 Finally bring up all the sides of the material and, using a fairly long piece of florist's wire, catch the material around the base of the arrangement. Trim any excess wire. Then take the ribbons and tie them in the traditional shoelace manner around the 'neck' of the arrangement. Tuck in the flaps of material all the way round the display.

BELOW: This bouquet can be rapidly turned into a lovely display by placing it in a fabric base and securing it with ribbons. Quick techniques like this make flower arranging a pleasure.

This makes a wonderful self-contained arrangement that needs no watering and no vase. Many other uses for this technique will no doubt occur to you. The convenience of using a piece of fabric cannot be ignored. Matching displays can be made for both ends of a sofa, or the fabric could be chosen to match the bedroom curtains.

STRAW HAT WITH LILAC

Decorated hats are not a new idea, we have been adorning our hats with natural things for many years. These hats can either be made as gifts to decorate the recipient's home or to be worn for special occasions.

Flowers: *1 stem trailing vine leaves in green/burgundy; 5 stems lilac flowers.*
Equipment: *straw hat; 1 m (1 yd) each, 5 cm (2 in) wide ribbon in lilac satin and green chiffon.*

This straw hat has actually been sprayed grey – dare I admit it with aerosol car spray paint? This works extremely well on straw, giving it a lovely shine rather than a gloss.

LEFT: This hat has a natural straw base and a grander selection of flowers, including gerbera, roses, larkspur, honesty and tiny blossoms. It would make a lovely gift or look fabulous for a wedding.

RIGHT: These two contrasting hats show some of the changes that can be made. They both have a similar base, it is just the flowers and paint colour that vary.

1 Make up a couple of bows in the same manner as described and illustrated on page 13 and glue the lilac bow on to the brim first, then nestle the green chiffon into the centre of the lilac ribbon.

2 Firmly attach one end of the trailing vine into the depths of the ribbon bows using a hot glue gun. Then wind the vine around the hat, trimming it so that the other end can be similarly stuck into the other side of the ribbons. Any leaves on the portion that you have trimmed off can be removed and glued directly on to the brim to thicken up the leaf garland around the brim.

3 Finally, trim the lilac stems very short and glue in the lilac flowers. If necessary dismantle some of the flowers into smaller pieces if the entire flower is too large. Make sure they are secured firmly on to the hat rather than gluing them to the leaves or ribbon.

1

2

3

A Gardener's Timepiece

Not a serious timepiece, more an amusing present for a super-keen gardener. It is fairly straightforward to purchase clock parts from major craft outlets. Alternatively, you could buy a plain, inexpensive clock and decorate that.

Flowers and vegetables: *3 sprays variegated geranium leaves; 2 stems lilac blossom; 3 miniature pumpkins.*
Equipment: *clock base; 2 x 2.5 cm (1 in) terracotta pots; 1 set of miniature garden tools.*

When you buy all the clock parts, you will find the base separate from the hands and the quartz mechanism. However, it does not take too long to assemble the whole kit and it feels very satisfying once you have got it all working. The miniature garden tools were purchased from a craft supplier. They should be moderately easy to find, but if you cannot, just use the vegetables and little terracotta pots which are widely available nowadays. Your choice of flowers can vary to include your favourite small leaves and blooms.

1 Start by attaching the variegated geranium leaves all around the clock as though the clock face was peeping through a growing geranium plant.

2 Glue on the pumpkins, one at a time as they need to be sturdily attached. Then firmly glue on the garden tools and terracotta pots.

3 Finally, fill any gaps with the dismantled florets from a lilac blossom; these blend well with the geranium leaves and add a very pretty finishing touch.

You could make alternative designs by decorating a similar shaped clock with rows of miniature terracotta pots filled with herbs or kitchen garden items. Pots of roses could look lovely, with trailing roses climbing around the clock face, and the pots could perhaps be whitewashed rather than left in their original terracotta colour. Other possibilities could be explored along the woodland theme with toadstools and wild plants or spring fever with masses of tulips and daffodils.

Right: Time for tea in the garden? This project, after a little concentration on clock assembly, is simple to make.

Floral Flowerpots

Attractive plant pots and plant pot holders are always welcome. Here some terracotta pots have been painted and then decorated with flowers, which makes them look very attractive when they are empty but doubly so when they have a plant nestling inside.

Flowers: *6–8 medium-sized ivy leaves; 3 sprays variegated geranium leaves; assorted flowers, here I have used pink pansies and white delphiniums.*

Equipment: *15 cm (6 in) terracotta pot, plain or painted.*

Make sure the surface of the pot is clean and dry. If it has been painted then make sure the paint is completely dry before starting to stick on the flowers.

1 Attach the ivy leaves in a small spray across the pot, leaving room in the middle for some flowers. Alternatively you could make a ring around the top lip of the pot or the base; any of these would look very effective.

2 Add some sprays of geranium leaves tucked in and around the ivy leaves. Many different types of foliage could be useful for this. As it takes such a small amount you may even have a few leaves left over from another project.

3 Finally, glue in the flowers, making them spread down from the top of the pot to the base. You can choose the variety of flowers by picking the recipient's favourite or using up odds and ends that you happen to have. A variety such as these small pansies are not very expensive to buy and are favourites for many people.

A decorated plant pot – perhaps together with a plant – could make an excellent gift for the hostess when you are visiting, or a birthday gift for a friend, or just a thank-you gift for a friend.

Right: This collection of decorated flower pots would make a marvellous selection of gifts for birthdays or Christmas. They are simple to make and very useful, especially if given with a plant inside.

DECORATED PHOTOGRAPH FRAMES

Plain photograph frames are fairly inexpensive and easy to track down from department and craft stores. Once they have been decorated with silk flowers they look very charming indeed.

Flowers: *spray of foliage – eucalyptus in this case; 8–9 daisies.*
Equipment: *plain picture frame approximately 30 cm (12 in) x 25 cm (10 in); ribbon or plaited string.*

As the frame shown here is plain pine or a similar wood, the plaited string gives a nice rustic accent to the design. If you were using a coloured frame then a ribbon might be more appropriate. You could, of course, paint or decorate a frame like this before you add the flowers, keeping in mind the photograph or picture the frame is intended to set off.

1 Make sure the frame is clean and free of grease. Then carefully stick the greenery on the bottom left hand corner. You can choose to put the spray of flowers in any position on the frame; it is purely a matter of personal taste. On the whole, however, the weight of the arrangement is better at the base of the frame, but whether it goes to the left or right is not important.

2 Glue in the daisies one by one, twist the stems a little to make sure that they have a little movement. This adds to the interest of the bunch.

3 Finally, glue on the last few flowers. Make up a bow from some plaited string, raffia or ribbon and place in the centre of the bunch. Add a few fake stalks to the base of the bunch to balance the visual effect, so that it looks as if the daisies are one bunch that has just been laid on the frame.

Other ideas will readily come to mind: a little spray of narcissi on a pale frame, or a spray of autumn leaves on a mahogany frame with a suitably autumnal photograph inside it, or a spray of wild roses on a wedding frame or silver anniversary frame. All these are simple ideas and projects that can be made in minutes and will give much pleasure.

BELOW: The sepia photograph adds to the romantic feel of the frame decorated with daisies. Adding flowers personalizes your gift.

RIGHT: Flowers complement your pictures.

Kitchen Storage

Recycled glass bottles are easily available all over the world now. They come in many sizes and designs and, by buying recycled glass, you may feel you are contributing a little to the 'Green' movement! The tiny artificial vegetables are made to such an amazingly high standard, they really do look just like the real thing!

Vegetables: *good selection of miniature vegetables, all shapes and sizes.*
Equipment: *3 recycled glass storage bottles.*

Although these bottles cry out to store olive oil and salad vinegars, you could also decorate larger or wider jars to match. Pasta jars could have a group of tomatoes on the cork, and beans and pulses could be kept in another vegetable decorated jar. Perhaps this would make an ideal gift for a vegetarian and certainly for an enthusiastic cook!

1 Begin by trying out your arrangement on the top of the bottle first. Place some fairly long vegetables across the corner of the jar, in this case asparagus, carrots and some cucumbers. It is essential that the longer vegetables are used at this stage as they will not fit in later. Before glueing them on, paint at least two coats of sealant across the shoulders of the jar. This will help to bond glue on to the shiny glass finish. Use a hot glue gun to fix these larger vegetables to the neck of the jar.

2 Gradually add some smaller and rounder ingredients such as garlic cloves, peppers and potatoes. The jars can have a random selection on each or a carefully planned, colour co-ordinated set.

3 Finally, fill the gaps with the smallest pieces that you have, in this case tomatoes, potatoes and aubergines. The arrangement should fill the neck of the bottle but not overwhelm the cork or the jars will be difficult to fill and pour.

RIGHT: These fascinating oil and vinegar bottles have been decorated with lovely miniature vegetables, which are beautifully made and great fun to work with. Matching jars and bottles are always a welcome present.

Red Roses for my Valentine

I would not suggest that the good thing about silk flowers is that you can make a Valentine gift once and then bring it out again year after year. But the versatility of silk flowers means there is far wider scope for making gifts that not only delight, but last as mementos of a special occasion.

Flowers: *5 large red roses.*
Equipment: *2 large twiggy hearts; 5 small twiggy hearts.*

This is the simplest of projects and takes only a few minutes to make but looks so pretty. The hearts are bought ready made, but if you have difficulty finding them, a similar design could be made with rings. Two large rings could be intertwined and some tiny wreaths used as decorations. You could also add ribbons if you wanted to. I felt these were so striking that ribbons would obscure the lines of the hearts.

1

2

3

Right: Gifts of flowers are the usual thing for Valentine celebrations. Here silk flowers are used to make a pretty decoration that could be made well in advance and would truly last for ever!

1 First bind the two large hearts together with a couple of strong pieces of stub wire. You can also help the wire along a little with some glue. Do not try to hold them together with glue on its own as it will not take the strain.

2 Next, glue on the leaves from the roses around the edge of the area on which the roses will be attached, to act as a backing for them.

3 Glue on the roses firmly, with three on the lower heart to keep more weight there than on the top one. As a final touch, add the small twiggy hearts between the roses at an angle so that they are nicely prominent and show up well; do not hide them away!

So many other things could be decorated with these lovely red roses. Gift boxes would need nothing but a few strands of ribbon and a couple of roses. A large gift could be boxed and wrapped with pretty lace paper and these intertwined hearts attached to the top as a decoration and second present.

The fascinating thing about this 'variety' of silk rose is that it actually has a tiny bit of blackspot painted on to it to make it slightly less than perfect as the majority of real roses are! A lovely touch!

Wooden Cornucopia

Jewellery, letters or just trinkets and keepsakes can all be kept in this unique box. The fabulous collection of fruit is attached individually and together looks quite wonderful. You could either collect the pieces bit by bit or buy them all at once.

Fruits: *30 or more wooden fruits in all shapes and sizes.*
Equipment: *wooden box; stain or paint if required.*

If you want to use a darker base, then stain the box before you start as it is difficult to cover all the wood once the fruit is attached. Although a slightly darker tone looks good, if you make it too dark it becomes more difficult to appreciate the fine shapes and carvings on the fruit.

1 Start with the lid of the box. Make sure that the surface is clean, dry and free of grease. Begin with the largest pieces that you have, here it is three pineapples, some grapes and a couple of half peaches. Glue them carefully on to the lid.

2 Next, add some more pieces and some smaller fruits to build a group of fruits nestling together. Try to avoid placing too many similar fruits near each other, aim for the greatest variety.

3 Finish the lid by adding some half or small-sized fruit to fill in any glaring gaps. It should not be possible to see the plain lid through the pile of fruit.

4 To decorate the front of the box, try to use pieces that are flatter in profile rather than very large round pieces like large pineapples. Glue them securely on to the box and make sure that they are all quite firmly fixed. You can then spray with aerosol varnish if you like, or paint with a slightly darker varnish, or paint with emulsion paint.

Right: This lovely box is probably too precious to give away as a present; perhaps you should keep it yourself! The wooden fruit look as though they have been carved with the box but they are all attached individually.

Credits

Managing Editor: Jo Finnis

Editor: Adèle Hayward

Designer: Jill Coote

Photographer: Di Lewis

Typesetting: SX Composing Ltd, Rayleigh, Essex

Production: Ruth Arthur; Sally Connolly;
Neil Randles; Karen Staff; Jonathan Tickner

Production Director: Gerald Hughes